SERMON OUTLINES

on

The Holy Spirit

The Bryant Sermon Outline Series

SERMON OUTLINES
on

The
Holy Spirit

compiled by
Al Bryant

kregel
PUBLICATIONS

Grand Rapids, MI 49501

Sermon Outlines on the Holy Spirit
compiled by Al Bryant

© 1998 by Kregel Publications

Published by Kregel Publications, a division of Kregel, Inc.,
P.O. Box 2607, Grand Rapids, MI 49501. Kregel Publications
provides trusted, biblical publications for Christian growth and
service. Your comments and suggestions are valued.

For more information about Kregel Publications, visit our web
site at: www.kregel.com

Cover design: Frank Gutbrod

Library of Congress Cataloging-in-Publication
Sermon outlines on the Holy Spirit / compiled by Al Bryant.
            p.   cm.
1. Holy Spirit—Sermons—Outlines, syllabi, etc. 2. Spiritual
life—Christianity—Sermons—Outlines, syllabi, etc.
I. Bryant, Al.
BT122.S48   1998   98-17622
231'.3—dc21

ISBN 0-8254-2057-1

2 3 4 5 / 04 03 02

Printed in the United States of America

CONTENTS

General Outlines on the Holy Spirit

PREFACE

I have chosen to divide this collection into three parts:

1. The Person and Work of the Holy Spirit
2. The Outworking of the Holy Spirit
3. General Outlines on the Holy Spirit

One might well describe this as the maturing process that must follow an infilling of the Holy Spirit. If a believer is not growing spiritually, he or she is like a stagnant pond. And stagnant ponds can become pretty horrible to contemplate and smell! While some of the outlines in the second section do not specifically expound the work of the Holy Spirit in the believer, they do show the "outworking" of the fruit of the Spirit in the believer.

I am indebted to many of the preachers of the past for these messages, and I hope they provide you, the user, with points to ponder and thoughts to build upon.

Al Bryant

The poems in this compilation are used by permission and taken from *Sourcebook of Poetry,* published in 1992 by Kregel Publications. The hymn lyrics are in public domain.

SCRIPTURE INDEX

THE HOLY SPIRIT: HIS PERSONALITY PROVEN

Galatians 3:2

1. He Speaks.

"Then the Spirit said unto Philip, Go near, and join thyself to this chariot" (Acts 8:29).

"While Peter thought on the vision, the Spirit said unto him, Behold, three men seek thee. Arise therefore, . . . and go with them, doubting nothing: for I have sent them" (Acts 10:19–20; cf. Acts 13:2; 1 Peter 1:11–12; 2 Peter 1:21).

2. He Teaches.

"But the Comforter, which is the Holy Ghost, whom the Father will send in my name, he shall teach you all things, and bring all things to your remembrance, whatsoever I have said unto you" (John 14:26; cf. Luke 12:12).

3. He Guides.

"Howbeit when he, the Spirit of truth, is come, he will guide you into all truth" (John 16:13; cf. Acts 11:12).

"For as many as are led by the Spirit of God, they are the sons of God" (Rom. 8:14).

4. He Forbids.

"Now when they had gone throughout Phrygia and the region of Galatia, and were forbidden of the Holy Ghost to preach the word in Asia, after they were come to Mysia, they assayed to go into Bithynia: but the Spirit suffered them not" (Acts 16:6–7).

5. He Reproves.

"And when he is come, he will reprove the world of sin, and of righteousness, and of judgment" (John 16:8).

6. He Testifies.

"But when the Comforter is come, whom I will send unto you from the Father, even the Spirit of truth, which proceedeth from the Father, he shall testify of me" (John 15:26; cf. John 16:14; Acts 20:23; Rom. 8:16).

7. He Appoints.

"As they ministered to the Lord, and fasted, the Holy Ghost said, Separate me Barnabas and Saul for the work whereunto I have called them" (Acts 13:2; cf. Acts 20:28).

8. He Sanctifies.

"Being sanctified by the Holy Ghost" (Rom. 15:16; cf. 1 Cor. 6:11).

9. He Comforts.

"And I will pray the Father, and he shall give you another Comforter, that he may abide with you for ever" (John 14:16; cf. Acts 9:31).

10. He Regenerates.

"That which is born of the flesh is flesh; and that which is born of the Spirit is spirit" (John 3:6; cf. Titus 3:5–6).

11. He Seals.

"And grieve not the Holy Spirit of God, whereby ye are sealed unto the day of redemption" (Eph. 4:30).

12. He Prays.

"Likewise the Spirit also helpeth our infirmities: for we know not what we should pray for as we ought: but the Spirit himself maketh intercession for us with groanings which cannot be uttered" (Rom. 8:26).

13. He Glorifies Christ.

"He shall glorify me: for he shall receive of mine, and shall show it unto you" (John 16:14).

14. He Ministers.

"For to one is given by the Spirit the word of wisdom; to another the word of knowledge by the same Spirit; . . . but all these worketh that one and the selfsame Spirit, dividing to every man severally as he will" (1 Cor. 12:8, 11).

15. He Baptizes.

"For by one Spirit are we all baptized into one body, whether we be Jews or Gentiles, whether we be bond or free; and have been all made to drink into one Spirit" (1 Cor. 12:13).

Treasures of Bible Truth

THE HOLY SPIRIT

Throughout the Scriptures the Holy Spirit is described and announced. He is:

1. **Coequal with Father and Son** (Gen. 1:2; Job 26:13; Ps. 33:6).

2. **Author of the Word** (1 Thess. 2:13; 2 Tim. 3:16; 1 Peter 20:21).

3. **Author of the Atonement** (Heb. 9:14).

4. **Author of the Resurrection** (1 Peter 3:18).

5. **Author of Spiritual Knowledge** (Luke 4:1–2; John 1:32–33; 3:5–6; 15:3; 16:8; Acts 13:3–5; 16:6–7; Rom. 8:15–16, 26–27; Eph. 1:13–14; 5:26; Heb. 2:17–18; 1 John 5:14).

L. W. Munhall

Blessed Quietness

Joys are flowing like a river since the comforter has come; He abides with us forever, makes the trusting heart His home.

Bringing life and health and gladness all around, this heav'nly guest banished unbelief and sadness, chang'd our weariness to rest.

Like the rain that falls from heaven, like the sunlight from the sky, so the Holy Ghost is given, coming on us from on high.

See, a fruitful field is growing, blessed fruit of righteousness; and the streams of life are flowing in the lonely wilderness.

What a wonderful salvation, where we always see His face! What a perfect habitation, what a quiet resting place!

Blessed quietness, holy quietness—what assurance in my soul! On the stormy sea He speaks peace to me—how the billows cease to roll!

Marnie P. Ferguson

THE PERSON AND WORK OF THE HOLY SPIRIT

Both the Old and New Testaments are clear in their descriptions of the Person and work of the Holy Spirit.

1. The Personality of the Holy Spirit Is Revealed.

a. In the Old Testament (Gen. 1:2; Job 26:13; Pss. 33:6; 104:30; Isa. 32:14–15; Ezek. 37:9).

b. In the New Testament (Matt. 3:15; 28:19; Mark 1:10; Luke 3:22; John 1:33; 1 Cor. 13:14; Eph. 4:30).

2. Character and Work of the Holy Spirit (John 14:16–26; 16:6–7; Rom. 8:26; 15:30; Acts 13:2).

a. Agent of Christ's birth (Matt. 1:18, 20; Luke 1:35; John 3:6; 1 John 5:6, 8).

b. Agent of the resurrection of Christ and of believers (Rom. 1:4; 8:11; 1 Peter 3:18).

3. From Whom the Spirit Proceeds (John 15:26; 16:7–14).

4. Dwelling of the Spirit in Christ (Luke 4:1, 14; John 3:34; Col. 2:9).

5. Regeneration by the Spirit (John 3:3, 5; 4:10, 14; 6:63; Titus 3:5, 7).

6. Dwelling of the Spirit in Believers (1 Cor. 2:9–16; 6:17; 12:13; Gal. 3:9; 4:6; 5:25; Eph. 2:22; 3:16; 5:1–18; 1 Peter 1:11; 1 John 3:24).

7. The Spirit Given to the Disciples (Acts 2:1–4; 6:3).

8. The Spirit to be Received by Faith (John 7:37–39; Luke 11:13; Gal. 3:2; Eph. 1:13–14).

9. Sanctification by the Spirit (Rom. 8:6; 1 Cor. 6:11; Gal. 5:22–26; 2 Thess. 2:13; 1 Peter 1:2).

10. The Spirit Dwelling in the Church (Rom. 8:9–11; 1 Cor. 3:16–17; 6:13–19; 2 Cor. 6:14–16; Eph. 1:22–23; 3:19; 4:12–16; Col. 1:18, 24; 1 Tim. 3:15; Heb. 3:6).

11. Prophesied in the Old Testament as a Gospel Blessing (Isa. 32:15; 44:3; Ezek. 36:27).

12. When the Dispensation of the Spirit Began and When It Will End (Matt. 3:11; John 7:39; 14:16; 15:26; 16:7; 20:22; Acts 1:8; 2:1–4; 3:21; 2 Thess. 2:7; Rev. 4:5).

13. Names and Titles of the Spirit.

a. Holy Spirit or Holy Ghost (Ps. 41:11; Isa. 63:11; Matt. 28:19; Mark 3:29; Luke 11:13).

b. Spirit of God (Gen. 1:2; Ex. 31:3; Num. 24:2; 1 Sam. 10:10; 2 Chron. 15:1; Matt. 3:16; 1 John 4:2).

c. My Spirit (Gen. 6:3; Prov. 1:23; Isa. 30:1; Zech. 4:6; Matt. 12:28).

d. Spirit of the Lord (Num. 11:29; Judg. 6:34; 2 Chron. 20:14; Acts 5:9).

e. Spirit of Christ (Rom. 8:9; 1 Peter 1:11).

f. The Comforter (John 14:16; 16:7).

g. Spirit of truth (John 14:17; 16:13).

h. Spirit of holiness (Rom. 1:4).

i. Spirit of grace (Zech. 12:10; Heb. 10:29).

j. Spirit of wisdom, might, counsel (Isa. 11:2).

k. Spirit of promise (Eph. 1:13).

l. Spirit of glory (1 Peter 4:14).

m. Good Spirit (Neh. 9:20; Ps. 143:10).

Selected

What the Holy Spirit Does in Us

The Holy Spirit within us is the security of our salvation; he is likewise an earnest of it, and assures our spirits that we have a title to eternal happiness. "The Spirit of God beareth witness with our spirits that we are the children of God." And in order that this inward testimony may be lively and permanent, it is absolutely necessary to attend carefully to the secret operation of the Holy Spirit within us; who, by infusing his holy consolations into our souls, by enlivening our drooping spirits, and giving us a quick relish of his promises, raises bright and joyous sensations in us, and gives a man, beforehand, a taste of the bliss to which he can look forward in heaven.

from *The John Wesley Reader*

BIBLICAL EMBLEMS OF THE HOLY SPIRIT

1. **Wind or Breath** (Song 4:16; Ezek. 37:9; John 3:8; 20:22; Acts 2:2).
    Mysterious, sovereign, mighty.

2. **Water** (Isa. 44:3; Ezek. 36:25; John 7:38–39).
    Pure, cleansing, refreshing, fertilizing, free.

3. **Fire** (Matt. 3:11).
    Penetrating, illuminating, warming, consuming.

4. **Oil** (Isa. 61:1; Heb. 1:9).
    Healing, comforting, consecrating.

5. **Seal** (Eph. 1:13; 4:30).
    Authenticating, making, securing.

6. **An Earnest** (Eph. 1:14).
    The pledge of future and full possession.

7. **A Dove** (Matt. 3:16).
    Gentle, peaceful, pure.

8. **A Guide** (John 16:13).
    Tender, faithful, unfailing.

Selected

Holy Ghost, with Light Divine

Holy Ghost, with light divine, shine upon this heart of mine; chase the shades of night away; turn my darkness into day.

Holy Ghost, with pow'r divine, cleanse this guilty heart of mine; long hath sin without control held dominion o'er my soul.

Holy Ghost, with joy divine, cheer this saddened heart of mine; bid my many woes depart; heal my wounded, bleeding heart.

Holy Spirit, all divine, dwell within this heart of mine; cast down ev'ry idol-throne; reign supreme and reign alone.

Andrew Reed

NAMES AND OFFICES OF THE HOLY SPIRIT

1. **The Names of the Holy Spirit.**
    Spirit (Eph. 5:18).
    Holy Spirit (Luke 11:3).
    Spirit of Truth (John 14:17).
    Spirit of Adoption (Rom. 8:15).
    Spirit of God (Rom. 8:9).
    Spirit of Christ (Rom 8:9).
    Spirit of Glory (1 Peter 4:14).
    Spirit of Grace (Heb. 10:29).
    Spirit of Promise (Eph. 1:13).
    Spirit of Wisdom (Eph. 1:17).
    Good Spirit (Neh. 9:20).
    Spirit of the Lord (Luke 4:18).
    Holy Ghost (Acts 1:5).
    Comforter (John 14:16).

2. **The Offices of the Holy Spirit.**
    Comforter (John 14:16).
    Teacher (John 14:26).
    Guide (John 26:13).
    Witness (Rom. 8:16).
    Intercessor (Rom. 8:26–27).
    Sanctifier (1 Cor. 6:11).
    Reprover (John 16:8).
    Revealer (Eph. 3:5).
    Giver (Rom. 5:5).
    Justifier (1 Cor. 6:11).
    Inspirer (2 Tim. 3:16).
    Author of Our Life (John 3:5–8).
    Quickener (1 Peter 3:18).
    Searcher (1 Cor. 2:10).
    Way of Access (Eph. 2:18).
    Renewer (Titus 3:5).

Selected

THE SPIRIT

Three dangerous ways in which people frustrate the Holy Spirit:

1. Resisting the Spirit.

Refusing to accept the testimony of Christ, as Acts 7:51, 53—the sin of the unconverted.

2. Grieving the Spirit.

Yielding to things forbidden, as Ephesians 4:29—the sin of the saints.

3. Quenching the Spirit.

Quenching the Spirit in others by despising prophesyings, that is, the Spirit speaking by others, as in 1 Thessalonians 5:19–20.

Selected

Breathe on Me, Breath of God

Breathe on me, Breath of God;
   Fill me with life anew,
That I may love what Thou dost love,
   And do what Thou wouldst do.

Breathe on me, Breath of God,
   Until my heart is pure,
Until with Thee I will one will—
   To do and to endure.

Breathe on me, Breath of God,
   Till I am wholly Thine,
Till all this earthly part of me
   Glows with Thy fire divine.

Breathe on me, Breath of God,
   So shall I never die,
But live with Thee the perfect life
   Of Thine eternity.

Edwin Hatch

THE OFFICE OR WORK OF THE HOLY SPIRIT

1. To Strive (Gen. 6:3; Acts 7:51).

2. To Send Forth (Ps. 104:30; John 15:26; Gal. 4:6).

3. To Move (Gen. 1:2).

4. To Speak (John 16:13; Acts 10:19; Rev. 22:17).

5. To Guide (John 16:13).

6. To Lead (Rom. 8:14).

7. To Help Our Infirmities (Rom. 8:26).

8. To Testify (Rom. 8:16; John 15:26).

9. To Reveal (Eph. 3:5).

10. To Search (1 Cor. 2:10).

11. To Possess a Mind (Rom. 8:27).

12. To Prophesy (John 16:13; 1 Tim. 4:1).

13. To Intercede (Rom. 8:26).

14. To Sanctify (1 Cor. 6:11).

15. To Quicken (John 6:63; 1 Peter 3:18).

16. To Be Pleased (Acts 15:28).

17. To Be Vexed (Isa. 63:10).

18. To Work in the Soul (Matt. 28:19; 1 Cor. 12:11; 2 Cor. 13:4; 1 Peter 1:20; 2 Peter 1:21).

Selected

THE WORK OF THE HOLY SPIRIT

1. **In Relation to the World He Is:**
   Creator (Gen. 1:26–27, with Job 33:4).
   Sovereign disposer of all things (1 Cor. 12:6, 11).

2. **In Relation to Christ's Kingdom He:**
   Raised Christ from the dead (Rom. 1:4; 1 Peter 3:18).
   Inspired the Scriptures (2 Tim. 3:16; 2 Peter 1:21).
   Convicts of sin (John 16:8–11).
   Regenerates (John 3:5–6; 1 John 5:4).
   Sanctifies (Rom. 15:16).
   Appoints and sends ministers (Matt. 9:38; Acts 13:2, 4; 20:28).
   Directs where they shall preach (Acts 16:6–7, 10).
   Witnesses concerning Christ (1 John 5:6; John 15:26).
   Edifies the church (Acts 9:31).

3. **In Relation to the Individual Saint He:**
   Witnesses to sonship (Rom. 8:16).
   Comforts (John 14:16).
   Imparts the love of God (Rom. 5:3–5).
   Imparts hope (Rom. 15:13; Gal. 5:5).
   Dwells in saints (John 14:17; 1 Cor. 3:16; 6:19).
   Is known by saints (John 14:17).
   Brings truth to remembrance (John 14:26).
   Guides into truth (John 16:13).
   Foreshows the future (John 16:13).
   Teaches (John 14:26).
   Gives power (Acts 1:8; Luke 24:49).
   Imparts spiritual gifts (1 Cor. 12:6–11).
   Helps our infirmities (Rom. 8:26).
   Shows how to answer persecutors (Mark 13:11; Luke 12:12).

Russell R. Byrum

BY MY SPIRIT

Zechariah 4:6

I. The Spirit the Only Source of Success.

II. On What Christ's Cause Does Not Depend.
   A. On human patronage or authority.
   B. On human force or the power of arms.
   C. On the carnal policy or the wisdom of men.
   D. On the riches, the learning, the eloquence of its friends.
   E. On moral or social standing.

III. The Cause of Christ Dependent upon the Spirit of God.
   A. The Spirit qualifies the instruments employed (1 Cor. 12:8)
   B. The Spirit makes the means effectual (1 Cor. 3:7).

IV. The Advantages Arising from This Arrangement.
   A. It keeps the church from despondency (Ps. 46:1–8).
   B. It insures success (Dan. 4:34).
   C. It gives all the glory to God. Who is Paul, or Cephas, or Apollos? (1 Cor. 1:26–31).

V. Implications of This Truth.
   A. Human instrumentality not excluded.
   B. The necessity of divine influence.
   C. The triumph of the church is certain. It has already survived the cruelty of Pharaoh, the combination of the Canaanitish kings, the fiery ordeal of a Herod and of a Nero, the bloodthirsty attacks of French infidelity and Nazi cruelty. It *is* standing now despite the subtle abuses of Modernism and other forms of anti-Christian cults and movements.

H. J. Appelman

THE HOLY SPIRIT AND CHRIST

If there is one thing more than another that is stated of the Lord Jesus, it is that in His life and labors, as the Man and Servant of God, He was dependent upon the Holy Spirit. In the Gospels and other New Testament passages there are no less than *fifteen* direct references to the Holy Spirit and His action in relation to the Lord Jesus, and *vice versa*.

1. Christ was **born** of the Holy Spirit as to His human nature (Matt. 1:18).

2. The Holy Spirit was the Father's promised **gift** to Christ (Matt. 12:18).

3. Christ was **sealed** with the Holy Spirit at His baptism (Mark 1:10).

4. The normal condition of Christ as to His life was that He was **full** of the Holy Spirit (Luke 4:1).

5. The Holy Spirit was the **sphere** in which Christ moved (Luke 4:14).

6. Christ was **led** by the Holy Spirit (Matt. 4:1).

7. The Holy Spirit was the **power** by which Christ exercised His ministry (Luke 4:18).

8. The Holy Spirit was the **energy** in which Christ overcame the powers of Satan (Matt. 12:28).

9. The Holy Spirit was the **secret** of Christ's joy (Luke 10:21).

10. The Holy Spirit was the **anointing** that enabled Christ to go about doing good (Acts 10:38).

11. The Holy Spirit was the **strength** that enabled Christ to offer Himself as a sacrifice to God on account of sin (Heb. 9:14).

12. The Holy Spirit was the **might** by which Christ was raised from the dead (Rom. 8:11).

13. The Lord Jesus was the **bestower** of the Holy Spirit to His disciples (John 20:22).

14. The Holy Spirit was the **authority** by which Christ gave His commands (Acts 1:2).

15. The Holy Spirit was the **justifier** of Christ (1 Tim. 3:16).

F. E. Marsh

The Spirit Glorifies Christ

He shall glorify me: for he shall take of mine, and shall declare it unto you (John 16:14 ASV).

To understand the work of the Holy Spirit, and truly experience it, one must try to grasp the relationship of the Holy Spirit to the Lord Jesus. Our Lord said definitely, before His departure, that the Spirit would come as a Comforter to the disciples. *The Spirit* would reveal Him in their hearts *in heavenly glory*. The disciples were full of the thought. They would not miss their Lord, but have Him with them always. This made them pray earnestly for the Holy Spirit, for they longed to have Jesus with them always. This was the promise of the Master: the Spirit should reveal Him to them.

This is the meaning of our text—"[The Spirit] shall glorify me [even as I am in the glory of heaven. He will make Me known]. He shall take of mine [My Love, My Joy, My Peace, and all My Life] and reveal it unto you." Where there is an earnest desire for the glory of Jesus in the heart of the believer, the Holy Spirit will preserve the holy presence of Jesus in our hearts all the day.

We must not weary ourselves with striving after God's presence. We must quietly endeavor to abide in fellowship with Christ always, to love Him and keep His commandments, and to do anything, in word and deed, in the name of Jesus. Then we will be able to count upon the secret but powerful working of the Spirit within us.

Andrew Murray in *Daily Secrets of Christian Living,*
published by Kregel Publications, 1996

SEVEN OFFICES OF THE SPIRIT

John, the Beloved Apostle, had much to say on the subject of the Holy Spirit. Among His offices he delineates the following:

1. **Quickening** (John 3:5–6; cf. John 1:12–13, 32–33).

2. **Indwelling** (John 4:14; cf. Eph. 4:30; 1 Thess. 5:19).

3. **Outflowing** (John 7:37–39).

4. **Comforting** (John 14:16–17; cf. Rom. 8:9; 1 Cor. 6:19; 1 John 2:1, 27).

5. **Teaching** (John 6:63; cf. John 14:26; Rom. 12:3; 1 Cor. 2:14; 8:2).

6. **Reproving** (John 16:8).

7. **Predicting** (John 16:13; cf. Matt. 1:18; 3:16; 12:28; Luke 4:1; Acts 2:33; 10:38; Rom. 8:11; Heb. 9:14).

Selected

The Dispensation of the Spirit

How much more shall your heavenly Father give the Holy Spirit to them that ask him? (Luke 11:13 ASV).

The writer of a little book on prayer tells us he has learned through his own experience the secret of a better prayer life, and would gladly pass on that which has helped him. As he was meditating on prayer, the great thought came with power, that we are now living in the dispensation of the Spirit. He says: "I feel deeply that in this time of the working of the Holy Spirit, all we may do in God's service is of little value unless it is inspired by the power of the Holy Spirit. This brought me to the well-known, precious, and inexhaustible text, 'How much more shall your heavenly Father give the Holy Spirit to them that ask him?'"

As I thought on this truth, I felt anew that the main thing for each of us is to receive, afresh from the Father, the Holy Spirit for our daily needs and daily life. Without this we cannot please God, nor can we be of any real help to our fellowmen. This brought the further thought that our prayers, if they are to raise our lives to fulfill God's purpose, must have their origin in God Himself, the highest source of power.

Andrew Murray in *Daily Secrets of Christian Living,*
published by Kregel Publications, 1996

WHAT THE COMFORTER SHALL DO

In his gospel, John, the apostle, quotes the words of Jesus as He promises to "send unto you from the Father" (John 15:26) the blessed Holy Spirit. The Holy Spirit:

1. Shall dwell with you and be with you (14:17).

2. Shall teach you all things (14:26).

3. Shall bring all things to your remembrance (14:27).

4. Shall testify you into all truth (15:26).

5. Will guide you into all truth (16:13).

6. Shall show you things to come (16:13).

7. Shall glorify me (16:14).

8. Shall take of mine and show it unto you (16:13).

Selected

Walking After the Spirit

They who "walk after the Spirit" (Gal. 5:16) are also led by Him into all holiness of conversation. Their "speech is always in grace, seasoned with salt," with the love and fear of God. "No corrupt communication comes out of their mouth, but only that which is good"; that which is "to the use of edifying"; which is "meet to minister grace to the hearers." And herein likewise do they exercise themselves day and night to do only the things which please God; in all their outward behavior to follow Him, "who left us an example that we might tread in his steps"; in all their relationships with their neighbor to walk in justice, mercy, and truth; and "whatsoever they do," in every circumstance of life, to "do all to the glory of God."

These are they who indeed "walk after the Spirit." Being filled with faith and with the Holy Spirit, they possess in their hearts, and show forth in their lives, in the whole course of their words and actions, the genuine fruits of the Spirit of God, namely, "love, joy, peace, longsuffering, gentleness, goodness, fidelity, meekness, temperance," and whatsoever else is lovely or praiseworthy. They "adorn in all things the gospel of God our Savior," and give full proof to all mankind, that they are indeed actuated by the same Spirit, "which raised up Jesus from the dead."

from *The John Wesley Reader*

WHAT THE HOLY SPIRIT DOES

John 3:5–6; 14:26; 16:8, 13
Romans 5:5; 14:17; 15:13
1 Corinthians 12:8
2 Corinthians 1:21–22; 3:17
1 John 2:17, 20, 28

Selected

Time

What, could ye not watch with me one hour? (Matt. 26:40 ASV).

Is it possible that Christians can say they cannot afford to spend a quarter or half an hour alone with God and His Word? When a friend comes to see us, or we have to attend an important meeting, or there is anything to our advantage or pleasure, we find time easily enough.

And God, the great God, who has a right to us and who in His wondrous love longs for us to spend time with Him that He may communicate to us His power and grace—we find no time for fellowship with Him. Even God's own servants, who might consider it their special privilege to be much with Him in prayer to receive the fullness of power—even His servants—are so occupied with their own work that they find little time for that which is all-important—waiting on God to receive power from on high.

Dear child of God, let us never say, "I have no time for God." Let the Holy Spirit teach us that the most important, the most blessed, the most profitable time of the whole day is the time we spend alone with God. Pray to the Lord Jesus, who in His earthly life experienced the need of prayer; pray to the Holy Spirit, who will impress upon us this divine truth. As indispensable to me as the bread I eat, and the air I breathe, is communion with God through His Word and prayer. Whatever else is left undone, God has the first and chief right to my time. Then only will my surrender to God's will be full and unreserved.

Andrew Murray in *Daily Secrets of Christian Living,*
published by Kregel Publications, 1996

THE HOLY SPIRIT THE COMFORTER

John 14:16; 20:22

I. His Work in Us.

A. Through Him we are chosen (1 Peter 1:2).

B. We are born again (John 3:5).

C. The love of God is shed abroad in our hearts (Rom. 5:5; Titus 3:5).

D. He is the power of God working in us (Phil. 1:6; 2:12–13).

E. He makes us the temples of God (1 Cor. 6:19; Eph. 2:22).

F. Conforms us to the likeness of His Son (2 Cor. 6:19; Eph. 2:22).

G. Purifies us (Acts 15:9).

H. Sanctifies us (1 Cor. 6:11).

I. Makes us fruitful (Gal. 5:22–26).

J. Witnesses in us (2 Cor. 1:21–22; Rom. 8:16).

II. His Work for Us.

A. He brings us into relationship with the heavenly Father (Rom. 8:14, 16).

B. Seals us unto the day of redemption (Eph. 4:30; 1:13).

C. Reveals the name of God to us (1 Cor. 2:10).

D. Brings us nigh to Him (Eph. 2:18).

E. Intercedes for us (Rom. 8:26–27).

F. Unfolds the Word (1 John 2:20, 27).

G. Instructs us (Luke 12:12; John 14:26).

H. Leads us into the truth (John 15:26; 1 Cor. 2:10).

I. Is a sure and certain guide (John 16:13).

J. Is our remembrance (John 14:26).

K. Comforts us (2 Cor. 5:5; Acts 9:31).

L. Strengthens us (Eph. 3:16; 2 Tim. 4:17).

M. Fills us with hope (Rom. 15:13; Gal. 5:5).

Handfuls of Help

THE SPIRIT OF TRUTH

The Spirit of truth . . . he will guide you into all truth (John 16:13).

This Spirit is the agent of God in the world today—living, eternal, universal.

I. The Message of the Spirit.

"The truth." The question is: Do we believe in the reality of the Spirit? This is fundamental to the right understanding of nature and grace.

Theory and practice are estranged in many philosophies of life. But knowing and doing are two sides of the same coin. Separation is destruction. Jesus linked them together in John 17:3, where the two essentials of religion are declared to be—to know God and to follow Christ.

II. The Method of the Spirit.

He will "guide" you. This word signifies movement and is true to what we know of the conditions in nature around us. Spiritual religion is not static but dynamic; it is not a machine, not a growing plant, not a law but an influence. So the Spirit of Truth will lead us out of our self-satisfied prejudices into the light of new knowledge and higher service that Christ's kingdom may come.

III. The Motive of the Spirit.

This has become clearer to us in our time through contrasting religion and science. The latter seeks facts and the former values.

The scientist must be informed, the worshiper consecrated. The Spirit of God therefore enters into life in order to teach us how to dedicate all the wisdom of man to the service of God.

Selected

SPIRITUAL LESSONS FROM THE LIFE OF ENOCH

Genesis 5:21–24; read Hebrews 12

I. **He Pleased God** (Heb. 11:5–6; see John 3:5–7; 8:29; Rom. 8:7–8). Things well pleasing to God:
   A. Presenting ourselves (Rom. 12:1).
   B. Doing good to others (Heb. 13:16).
   C. Not conformed to the world (Rom. 12:2).
   D. Christian benevolence (Phil. 4:18).
   E. Manifesting the fruit of the Spirit (Eph. 5:8–10).
   F. Obedience to parents (Col. 3:20).
   G. Whole life devoted to Him (2 Cor. 5:9).

II. **He Walked with God** (Gen. 5:22, 24).
   A. Walked—*Progress.*
   B. Walked with—*Companionship.*
   C. Walked with God—*Privilege.* The highway of holiness. The first step down and out of self. The humble shall be exalted. See Psalm 1:1; Amos 3:3; 2 Corinthians 6:14; Ephesians 2:1–3; Revelation 3:4.

III. **He Witnessed for God** (Jude 14:15). No man can give faithful testimony who is not pleasing God and walking with Him. See Proverbs 4:5; Luke 24:48; Acts 1:8.
   A. Enoch's end (Heb. 11:5).
   B. Please God. Cannot please world.
   C. Walk with God. Cannot walk with world.
   D. Testify for God. Cannot testify for the world. See Colossians 1:10.

S. R. Briggs

BLESSINGS THAT COME TO THE MEEK

Meekness, or "gentleness," is another of those often misunderstood facets of the fruit of the Spirit. It is worthy of a closer look.

1. **Satisfaction.** "The meek shall eat and be satisfied" (Ps. 22:26).

2. **Discretion.** "The meek will he guide in judgment" (Ps. 25:9).

3. **Instruction.** "The meek will he teach his way" (Ps. 25:9).

4. **Salvation.** "Save all the meek of the earth" (Ps. 76:9).

5. **Exaltation.** "The LORD lifteth up the meek" (Ps. 147:6).

6. **Beautification.** "He will beautify the meek" (Ps. 149:4).

7. **Valuation.** "A meek and quiet spirit" (1 Peter 3:4).

F. E. Marsh

Gracious Spirit

Gracious Spirit, dwell with me;
   I myself would gracious be;
And with words that help and heal
   Would Thy life in mine reveal;
And with actions bold and meek
Would for Christ my Saviour speak.

Truthful Spirit, dwell with me;
   I myself would truthful be;
And with wisdom kind and clear
Let Thy life in mine appear;
   And with actions brotherly
   Speak my Lord's sincerity.

Holy Spirit, dwell with me;
   I myself would holy be;
Separate from sin, I would
Choose and cherish all things good,
   And whatever I can be
Give to Him who gave me Thee!

Thomas Toke Lynch

BLESSED ONES

The word *blessed* in the following passages means "happy." The soul of happiness may be summarized as contentment, peace, and joy—all gifts of the Holy Spirit.

The blessed or happy ones are those:

1. "Whose **robes** are washed in the Blood of the Lamb" (Rev. 22:14 RV).

2. Whose **iniquities** are forgiven through God's grace (Rom. 4:7–8).

3. Who **obey** Christ's Word to minister to others (John 13:17).

4. Who **endure** temptation by getting the victory (James 1:12).

5. Who **give** of their substance rather than receive (Acts 20:35).

6. Who **have not seen** Christ, and yet believe in Him (John 20:29).

7. Who **fulfill** the conditions embodied in the twelve Blesseds of Christ found in Matthew's gospel (5:3–11; 11:6; 13:16; 24:46).

F. E. Marsh

Drought

My heart is parched by unbelief,
    My spirit sere from inward strife;
The heavens above are turned to brass,
    Arid and fruitless is my life.

Then falls Thy rain, Oh Holy One;
    Fresh is the earth, and young once more;
Then falls Thy Spirit on my heart;
    My life is green; the drought is o'er!

Betty Bruechert

ABIDE

As the branch cannot bear fruit of itself, except it abide in the vine; no more can ye, except ye abide in me (John 15:4).

"The most beautiful thing to St. John," said George Mattheson, "was abidingness." It all depends, of course, where we abide, but the word itself has peace at the heart of it and contentment and power.

I. Only Those Who Abide in Me, Said Jesus, Reap the Rich Harvests of the Spirit.

For the best fruits of life ripen but slowly and are to be had only as we continue in those estates of body, mind, and soul that make them possible.

A. Love needs to be long dwelt with to do its perfect work.

B. Truth must be our constant comrade to have its sustaining way with us.

C. Goodness must be given an abiding and unhindered opportunity before the rare and finished beauty of it ripens in character or conduct. Only unbroken communion with God makes a Godlike life. Nothing comes of a life that is constantly uprooting itself.

II. To Whom the Command Is Given; to Those Already in Him.

By knowledge of Him.
By faith in Him.
By love to Him.
By union with Him.

III. The Promise Made to Those Who Abide in Christ and Advantages Resulting.

Christ will abide in us by His Word, teaching, directing, strengthening, supporting, comforting us. By His indwelling presence as the Holy Spirit, permitting us to have fellowship with Him. There is a call to conscious vital union with our Lord, which comes only from a Spirit-led walk with Him.

Selected

"LETS" THAT LET IN A BLESSING

1. **Vigilance.** "Let your loins be girded about" (Luke 12:35).

2. **Diligence.** "Let every man prove his own work" (Gal. 6:4).

3. **Continuance.** "Let us not be weary in well doing" (Gal. 6:9).

4. **Dominance.** "Let the peace of God rule in your hearts" (Col. 3:15).

5. **Sustenance.** "Let the word of Christ dwell in you richly" (Col. 3:16).

6. **Endurance.** "Let us run with patience the race" (Heb. 12:1).

7. **Supplication.** "Let your requests be made known unto God" (Phil. 4:6).

8. **Utterance.** "Let your speech be always with grace" (Col. 4:6).

F. E. Marsh

Jesus Calls Us

Jesus calls us o'er the tumult of our life's wild, restless sea; day by day His sweet voice soundeth, saying, "Christian, follow Me."

Jesus calls us from the worship of the vain world's golden store, from each idol that would keep us, saying, "Christian, love Me more."

In our joys and in our sorrows, days of toil and hours of ease, still He calls, in cares and pleasures, "Christian, love Me more than these."

Jesus calls us: by Thy mercies, Savior, may we hear Thy call, give our hearts to Thy obedience, serve and love Thee best of all.

Mrs. Cecil F. Alexander

"Go home" (Mark 5:19) "and shew how great things God hath done unto thee" (Luke 8:39). It is there that the fruit of the Spirit must be most evident.

It is in the home we need to have:

1. **Our speech** seasoned with the salt of grace, that we may speak sweetly (Col. 4:6).

2. **Our manners** tempered with the grace of courteousness, that we may act graciously (1 Peter 3:8).

3. **Our behavior** toned with the godliness of chastity, that we may attract powerfully (1 Peter 3:1–2).

4. **Our conduct** tuned with the Word of God, that we may act consistently (Titus 2:1–14).

5. **Our rule** ruled with the authority of heaven, that we may behave consecratingly (1 Tim. 3:1–7).

6. **Our office** dominated with the beauty of faithfulness, that we may live blamelessly (1 Tim. 3:8–13).

7. **Our relations** in life adjusted with the direction of the Spirit, that we may show we have received the Spirit fully (Col. 3:17; 4:1; Eph. 5:18; 6:9).

F. E. Marsh

The Secret of Shining

The moment the Spirit of the Almighty strikes the heart of him who was until then without God in the world, it breaks the hardness of his heart, and creates all things new. The Sun of Righteousness appears and shines upon his soul, showing him the light of the glory of God in the face of Jesus Christ. He is in a new world. All things around him are become new, such as it never before entered into his heart to conceive.

He sees that he has "an advocate with the Father, Jesus Christ the righteous," and that he has "redemption in his blood, the remission of sins." He sees "a new way that is opened into the holiest by the blood of Jesus," and his light "shineth more and more unto the perfect day."

from *The John Wesley Reader*

BARNABAS—FULL OF THE SPIRIT

Acts 11:22–24

Evidences of being full of the Spirit.

1. **A Seeing Eye.** "Had seen the grace of God."

2. **A Glad Heart.** "Was glad."

3. **A Ready Foot.** "He came."

4. **A Helpful Tongue.** "Exhorted them all."

5. **A True Character.** "He was a good man."

6. **A Consecrated Man.** "Full of the Holy Ghost" (see Acts 4:36–37).

7. **A Believing Soul.** "Full . . . of faith."

F. E. Marsh

The Joyful Sound

Blessed is the people that know the joyful sound: They walk, O Jehovah, in the light of thy countenance. In thy name do they rejoice all the day (Ps. 89:15–16 ASV).

"Glad tiding of great joy" was what the angel calls the Gospel message. This is what is here spoken of as "the joyful sound." That blessedness consists in God's people walking in the light of God and rejoicing in His name all the day. Undisturbed fellowship, never-ending joy is their portion. Even in the Old Testament such was at times the experience of the saints. But there was no continuance; the Old Testament could not secure that. Only the New Testament can and does.

In every well-ordered family one finds the father delighting in his children and the children rejoicing in their father's presence. And this mark of a happy home on earth is what the heavenly Father has promised and delights to work in His people—*walking in the light of His countenance, and rejoicing in His name all the day.* It has been promised, it has been made possible in Christ through the Holy Spirit filling the heart with the love of God. It is the heritage of all who are seeking to love God with all their heart and strength.

Andrew Murray in *Daily Secrets of Christian Living,*
published by Kregel Publications, 1996

BELIEVER'S ATTITUDE

To the doctrine (teaching) of the Holy Spirit.

1. Continue in it **steadfastly**, as wholehearted believers in Christ (Acts 2:42).

2. Be shaped by it **continually** as pliable saints (Rom. 6:17).

3. Feed upon it **personally** as dependent disciples (1 Tim. 4:16).

4. Attend to it **regularly** as diligent scholars (1 Tim. 4:13).

5. Take heed to it **thoroughly** as earnest stewards (1 Tim. 4:16).

6. Teach it **faithfully** as consistent doers (1 Tim. 6:3; Titus 2:7, 10).

7. Preach it **tenaciously** as zealous workers (2 Tim. 4:2; Titus 2:1).

8. Hold it **firmly** as convinced witnesses (Titus 1:9; 2 John 10).

9. Abide in it as **satisfied** servants (2 John 9).

F. E. Marsh

Trusting Jesus

Simply trusting ev'ry day, trusting thru a stormy way; even when my faith is small, trusting Jesus—that is all.

Brightly does His Spirit shine into this poor heart of mine; while He leads I cannot fall, trusting Jesus—that is all.

Singing if my way is clear, praying if the path be drear, if in danger, for Him call, trusting Jesus—that is all.

Trusting as the moments fly, trusting as the days go by; trusting Him whate'er befall, trusting Jesus—that is all.

Edgar Page Stiles

ALL-NESS OF THE CHRISTIAN LIFE

How many of God's people know the fullness of blessing found in connection with the little word "all" in the following Scriptures?

1. God has blessed us with "**all** spiritual **blessings** . . . in Christ" (Eph. 1:3).

2. He has "given . . . **all things** that pertain unto life and godliness" (2 Peter 1:3).

3. He is able to make "**all grace** abound toward you" (2 Cor. 9:8).

4. "**All** the **promises** of God are in [Christ] yea, and in him Amen " (2 Cor. 1:20).

5. He desires we should be filled into "**all**" His **fullness** (Eph. 3:19).

6. He can supply "**all**" our **need**, according to His riches in Christ Jesus (Phil. 4:19).

7. He assures us "**all things**" are ours (1 Cor. 3:21–22).

F. E. Marsh

All the Way My Savior Leads Me

All the way my Savior leads me; what have I to ask beside? Can I doubt His tender mercy, who through life has been my Guide? Heavenly peace, divinest comfort, here by faith in Him to dwell! For I know whate'er befall me, Jesus doeth all things well.

All the way my Savior leads me, cheers each winding path I tread, gives me grace for ev'ry trial, feeds me with the living bread. Though my weary steps may falter, and my soul athirst may be, gushing from the Rock before me, lo! a spring of joy I see.

All the way my Savior leads me; Oh, the fullness of His love! Perfect rest to me is promised in my Father's house above. When my spirit, clothed immortal, wings its flight to realms of day, this my song through endless ages: Jesus led me all the way.

Fanny J. Crosby

PENTECOST AFTERMATH
(POST-PENTECOST)

And they continued stedfastly in the apostles' doctrine and fellowship,
and in breaking of bread, and in prayers (Acts 2:42).

We have here a beautiful picture of primitive church life in its simplicity, its purity, and its fidelity.

1. First, They Remained Loyal—"continued stedfastly."

There was nothing weak or wavering about these early Christians. But they used means. They placed safeguards about their Christian profession.

2. One of These Safeguards Was the Study of Doctrine— "They continued stedfastly in the apostles' doctrine."

There was much for them to learn. It is the glory of Christianity that it is a teaching religion. It offers men an open Bible, an open church, an open way of redemption, and an open means of access to God.

Those early Christians were the first learners. Their Christian education was not confined to one portion of their life. Truth was added to truth. Light increased to greater light.

The quiet teaching of the great truths of God is one of the greatest blessings of religion. If we are to attain to right views of God, right views of ourselves, right views of the world, we must study doctrine.

3. They Maintained Good Fellowship.

This was another safeguard of their spiritual life. They lived in an age of hostility. This drew them into close spiritual association. In fellowship they found a powerful means of sustaining their common spiritual life.

4. They Remembered Christ's Sufferings—"[they] continued in breaking of bread."

An important safeguard to the Christian life is faithful observance of Christian ordinances.

5. Prayer Was Another Safeguard They Threw About Their Spiritual Life.

The early Christians didn't neglect prayer. They did not theorize about prayer; they prayed. They continued in prayer. They found help in communion with Christ.

"Prayers." There were public prayers, too. A life of prayers was to them a life of happiness and strength.

Hallock

Come, Holy Spirit, Heavenly Dove

Come, Holy Spirit, heavenly Dove,
  With all Thy quick'ning powers;
Kindle a flame of sacred love
  In these cold hearts of ours.

Look, how we grovel here below,
  Fond of these trifling toys:
Our souls can neither fly nor go
  To reach eternal joys.

In vain we tune our formal songs,
  In vain we strive to rise:
Hosannas languish on our tongues,
  And our devotion dies.

Dear Lord, and shall we ever live
  At this poor, dying rate?
Our love so faint, so cold, to Thee,
  And Thine to us so great?

Come, Holy Spirit, heavenly Dove,
  With all Thy quick'ning powers;
Come, shed abroad a Saviour's love,
  And that shall kindle ours.

Isaac Watts

THE HOLY SPIRIT'S WORK IN US

He shall testify of me (John 15:26).

An important part of the Holy Spirit's great work is to testify of Christ.

1. He testifies of the value of Christ's sacrifice.

2. He testifies to the prevalence of His intercession.

3. He testifies as to the dimensions of His love.

4. He testifies of the suitableness and sufficiency of His salvation.

5. He testifies of the beauty and glory of His person and character.

We believers are to hear, heed, and appropriate the Holy Spirit's testimony.

Selected

Where there is much traffic of bad thinking, there will be much mire and dirt. Every wave of wicked thought adds something to the corruption which rots upon the shore of life. It is dreadful to think that a vile imagination, once indulged, gets the key of our minds, and can get in again very easily, whether we will it or not. Thus, it can so return as to bring seven other spirits with it more wicked than itself. And what may follow, no one knows.

C. H. Spurgeon

THE HOLY SPIRIT—IN HIS DIVINE OPERATIONS

And it shall come to pass in the last days, saith God, I will pour out of my Spirit upon all flesh: and your sons and your daughters shall prophesy, and your young men shall see visions, and your old men shall dream dreams (Acts 2:17).

We have considered briefly the Holy Spirit in His divine personality, His general work, His miraculous operations, etc., and in His free and universal influences. We shall be much assisted if we look now at some special aspects of the Holy Spirit given to us.

I. As the Result of the Savior's Sacrifice and Work.

Hence, Jesus was to send the Holy Spirit. He was to baptize with the Holy Spirit and with fire. He was given and poured out as the result of Messiah's work. Thus the magnificent passage—"Thou hast ascended on high, thou hast led captivity captive" (Ps. 68:18), etc. So the Holy Spirit took Christ's place in the church and was to abide forever. The ascension of the one, the descent of the other. The going away of Christ, and the coming of the Spirit.

II. Notice the Blessings the Holy Spirit Brings to Believers.

He is poured out, given, sent. But He must be received—accepted, and become ours. This only by faith and prayer. "If ye," etc.

A. He is the Spirit of holiness to sanctify, so constantly called the Holy Spirit, as He cleanses, transforms.

B. He is the witness within of our acceptance with God. "The Spirit . . . beareth witness" (Rom. 8:16).

C. He is the seal of our sonship (see 2 Cor. 1:22).

D. He is the pledge of all good—called "The earnest" (2 Cor. 1:22).

E. He is the anointer for all Christian offices (2 Cor. 1:22; 1 John 2:20, 27).

F. He is the perfecter of the divine work in the soul—establishes, builds up, teaches, guides, makes us meet, etc. Hence, "He is the Spirit of worship, of prayer," of praise (Jude 20).

III. Some of the Symbols by Which the Holy Spirit Is Represented.

A. As the *vital air* or *wind*. "Valley of dry bones," etc. Christ to Nicodemus. No life without it. So the winds scatter miasma, etc.

B. As the *rain* and the *dew*. I will be as the dew, etc. Where there is no rain there is no fertility—beauty, etc. "Showers" come down as the rain. "He that believeth in me." "So I would have given," etc. "Let Him take of the waters," etc.

C. As the *fruit* of the *vine,* and as *milk* (Isa. 55).

D. As *oil*. "Oil of gladness." The consecrating oil of the king and of the priest. Softening, beautifying, cooling, healing.

E. He is compared to *fire*. "Holy Ghost and fire," so an Old Testament prophecy in Isaiah 4:5. "Quench not the Spirit." "Stir up the gift." "Fire on the altar," etc.

IV. The Spirit We Should Seek to Live Out with Regard to the Holy Spirit.

A. *Deep humility*. How unworthy. "What condescension."

B. *Entire dependence*. He is to be our light and strength, our defense, guide, guard.

C. *Constant believing* prayer. Pray for Him. By His aid we pray, seek His presence.

D. Holy *tranquillity* and *joy*. Righteousness, peace, and joy in the Holy Spirit.

E. Our abiding Comforter in all our *trials* and *sorrows*.

F. Ever to be extolled and glorified by us. Exhort to a closer recognition of the Holy Spirit. We all need it—the whole church, and all others.

Jabez Burns

Every disciple of Jesus Christ who desires to take part in the victory that overcomes the world needs time and faith and the Holy Spirit to come under the full conviction that it is as the servant of the omnipotent Lord Jesus that he is to take his part in the work. He is to count literally upon the daily experience of being "strong in the Lord and in the power of his might." The word of promise gives the courage to obey implicitly the word of command.

Andrew Murray

THE SPIRIT POURED OUT

And it shall come to pass in the last days, saith God, I will pour out of my Spirit upon all flesh (Acts 2:17).

By the Spirit is meant the Holy Spirit of God, the Third Person of the blessed Trinity. The personality of the Spirit is as constantly taught as the personality of the Father or the Son. He is invariably spoken of as a person. He is associated with the Father and the Son in the work of creation, providence, and redemption. Yet in the economy of our salvation, He has a distinct office and work, as distinct from the gracious purposes of the Father or the mediatorial work of the Son.

Jesus, in concluding His mission on earth, indicates the coming of the Holy Spirit as His special gift, as the Convincer of sin and the Comforter of His people, and assures them of the absolute certainty that He will come to them.

And now the way is opened for His wondrous descent. Jesus has died, risen again, and ascended to the Father, the disciples are waiting for the promised Paraclete, and on the fiftieth day, the Pentecost celebration, the Feast of Weeks and of Harvest, the Spirit descends in all His plenitude and power. The account is most minutely given, and as the abiding Divine Presence in the church, He becomes the guide, the sanctifier, and consolation of believers.

Notice,

I. The Divine Spirit Has Executed His Divine Power from the Beginning.

A. He worked with His strong operations in the preaching of Noah.

B. He was eminently manifested in raising up God's servants to do His special work—i.e., Moses, Aaron, Caleb, Deborah, Samson, Gideon, Jephtha, Saul, etc.

C. He inspired the holy men of old to reveal the will of God in the Holy Scriptures (Heb. 1:1).

D. He endowed people for great and extraordinary duties—people like Elijah, Elisha, Zerrubbabel, Nehemiah, Simeon, Anna, John the Baptist, etc.

E. He inaugurated the Savior, and testified to His divine person and work (Matt. 3:16–17).

F. By His might He vanquished the Devil in the wilderness (Matt. 4:10).

G. So Jesus, also, in His miracles put forth the power of the Spirit of God that dwelt fully in Him. Here we have the distinctly marked course of the Holy Spirit from the earliest records of Bible times. But now,

II.   He Was Given to the New Testament Church.
And thus,

A. Ancient prophecies were fulfilled.

B. The needs of the church supplied. The holy oracles had long been silent, the Messiah had ascended, and the Holy Spirit came down to supply the bereaved and sorrowing church.

C. The messiahship and glory of Christ were thus attested; here was the sign, the witness, the seal of the divinity of Jesus and of His finished earthly work.

D. By Him the needed gifts and power were bestowed on the apostles and disciples of Jesus. Thus they had burning, flaming tongues, power for their arduous and onerous work. He came to inspire with knowledge and wisdom and zeal and courage and eloquence.

E. By Him success was given to the divine means employed. For conviction—for conversion, sanctification. He is the illuminator, the regenerator, the indwelling witness, the guide and leader to eternal glory.

Jabez Burns

Fill Me Now

Hover o'er me, Holy Spirit,
　Bathe my trembling heart and brow;
Fill me with Thy hallowed presence,
　Come, O come and fill me now.

Thou canst fill me, gracious Spirit,
　Though I cannot tell Thee how;
But I need Thee, greatly need Thee,
　Come, O come and fill me now.

I am weakness, full of weakness,
　At Thy sacred feet I bow;
Blest, divine, eternal Spirit,
　Fill with pow'r, and fill me now.

Cleanse and comfort, bless and save me,
　Bathe, O bathe my heart and brow;
Thou art comforting and saving,
　Thou art sweetly filling now.

E. R. Stokes

THE OPENED EYES

I am sending you to them to open their eyes and turn them from dark-
ness to light (Acts 26:17–18 NIV).

The analogy between the bodily senses and the mental and moral faculties is most striking. The soul has its organs of vision as well as the body—there are spiritual eyes as well as natural, and to these our subject refers. Let us then consider, in reference to the text,

I. The Condition Supposed.

Eyes closed—blind—in moral and spiritual darkness.

A. This blindness is *natural.* Man's normal condition—he is so from his birth. It is the result of his fallen and depraved condition. Like the young man in the Gospel—blind from birth.

B. This *darkness* relates to all *spiritual things.* To God and His attributes—to the divine law and its claims—to man's carnal and evil nature—to the Gospel and the claims of Christ. In one word, to all things connected with the spiritual and divine. See it fully stated in 1 Corinthians 2:11, and following.

C. This *blindness* is *obvious* in the character and life. The thoughts and words and conduct evidence this blindness, this want of holy, saving light.

D. This *blindness* is a *condition* of *wretchedness* and *peril.* How pitiable natural blindness, how much more the darkness of the soul. The fruit is bitter—the end death.

E. It is *incurable* by *human agency.* Learning of any kind, philosophy, science, art, have all failed—the world with all its wisdom knew not God, nor the way of peace, nor of the world to come—that is clearly and distinctly true.

Now see,

II. The Divine Instrumentality for Opening Blind Eyes.

A. There is the *living agent.* "I send thee." Paul the apostle—the preacher—he raises up the ministry of the Gospel for this end—for this work.

B. There is the *word* of *light* and *power.* The Gospel, God's word is the omnific fiat, commanding light to be, and removing the darkness of the soul. See how expressly it is stated in 2 Corinthians 4:4, 6. "The entrance of [the Divine] word giveth light . . ." (Ps. 119:130).

C. The *enlightening influence* is of the *Spirit* of God. The Holy Spirit takes away the films, gives to sightless eyes the power to see, and then floods the soul with the saving knowledge of the Lord Jesus Christ. He takes of the things of Christ, and makes them evident and saving to the soul. We have this threefold agency in all spiritual work—the Gospel, the preacher, and the essential power of the Holy Spirit—or the Holy Spirit doing this gracious enlightening work by the ministry of the Gospel.

Application

Let the subject lead:

A. To an appeal to all present as to their condition of blindness or sight.

B. To the preacher as to his obvious work, to open blind eyes.

C. As to the progress of the church for this preaching of the Gospel, being crowned with the presence and power of the Holy Spirit.

Jabez Burns

Open My Eyes

Open my eyes, that I may see glimpses of truth Thou hast for me; place in my hands the wonderful key that shall unclasp and set me free. Silently now I wait for Thee, ready, my God, Thy will to see; open my eyes—illumine me, Spirit divine!

Open my ears, that I may hear voices of truth thou sendest clear; and while the wave-notes fall on my ear, ev'rything false will disappear. Silently now I wait for Thee, ready, my God, Thy will to see; open my ears—illumine me, Spirit divine!

Open my mouth, and let me bear gladly the warm truth ev'rywhere. Open my heart and let me prepare love with Thy children thus to share. Silently now I wait for Thee, ready, my God, Thy will to see; open my heart—illumine me, Spirit divine!

Clara H. Scott

THE SPIRIT-FILLED CHRISTIAN

And they were all filled with the Holy Ghost, and began to speak with other tongues, as the Spirit gave them utterance (Acts 2:4).

The whole book of Acts is radiant with the stories of those whose souls were filled with the Spirit, and shows us the glorious effect of the Holy Spirit's indwelling in the lives of the early disciples. Four examples:

1. **Peter**—Ease and boldness in speech; unswerving fidelity to Christ.

2. **Stephen**—Angelic sweetness and patience, courageous testimony, heroic fortitude.

3. **Philip**—Persuasive reasoning and patient persistence in winning individual souls to Christ.

4. **Paul**—Splendid consecration in giving up his high social status and casting in his lot with the despised Nazarenes, and devoting his great talents to the service of Christ.

J. Ellis

The story of the birth of the church in the outpouring of the Holy Spirit, and of the first freshness of its heavenly life in the power of that Spirit, will teach us how *prayer on earth,* whether as cause or effect, *is the true measure of the presence of the Spirit of heaven.* As little as the power of the Spirit could be given without Christ sitting on the throne, *could it descend without the disciples on the footstool of the throne.* For all the ages the law is laid down here at the birth of the church, that whatever else may be found on earth, the power of the Spirit must be prayed down from heaven. The measure of believing, continued prayer will be the measure of the Spirit's working in the church. Direct, determined, definite prayer is what we need.

At Samaria, Philip had preached with great blessing, and many had believed. But the Holy Spirit, as yet, was fallen on none of them. The apostles send down Peter and John to pray for them, that they might receive the Holy Spirit. The power for such prayer was a higher gift than preaching, the work of the men who had been in closest contact with the Lord of glory, the work that was essential to the perfection of the life that preaching and baptism, faith and conversion, had only begun. Surely of all the gifts of the early church for which we should long there is none more needed than the gift of prayer—prayer that brings down the Holy Spirit on believers. This power is given to the men who will say: "We will give ourselves to prayer."

Andrew Murray

HOLY SPIRIT'S COUNTERACTING WORK

The law of the Spirit of life in Christ Jesus hath made me free from the law of sin and death (Rom. 8:2).

"Professor Lefroy, of the Imperial College of Science and Technology, has devised a solution expected to put an end to the ravages of the 'death watch' beetle," pointed out the London correspondent in an old edition of the Yorkshire Post.

"This little creature, only a quarter of an inch long, spends its life burrowing about in old woodwork, until the infected wood becomes riddled and rotten. Its familiar ticking sound is produced by a small club-shaped extension of the antenna, with which it knocks on any surrounding woodwork in order to call its mate.

"Many old buildings embodying wooden beams and rafters have been endangered by this beetle's tireless activities. Lincoln Cathedral, where the woodwork supporting the roof has been seriously attacked, is a notable example.

"Professor Lefroy's solution is built up from a white, sweet-smelling substance known as paradichlorobenzine. Certain oils are added to this, and the resulting mixture is sprayed on the affected surfaces. The mixture gradually sinks into the wood, poisoning the beetles inside, and so permeates the wood that fresh beetles are prevented from working their way in."

The solution is destructive and preventative: killing the beetle, and preventing others from working their way into the wood. This is what the Holy Spirit does in the heart and life of the believer in Christ. If Romans 8 is carefully and prayerfully pondered, it will be seen He destroys sin and prevents from sin. The Holy Spirit is:

1. The **Liberator** from the law of sin and death (v. 2).

2. The **Leader** guiding the believer toward things of Himself (vv. 4–5).

3. The **Life** of the new nature (vv. 9–12).

4. The **Guide** who leads us in the ways of life (v. 14).

5. The **Witness** to assure of our relationship (v. 16).

6. The **Earnest** of the glorified body (v. 23).

7. The **Intercessor** in the prayer life (vv. 26–27).

F. E. Marsh

LED BY THE SPIRIT

For as many as are led by the Spirit of God, they are the sons of God (Rom. 8:14).

Wonderful leadership. His children are led by the Spirit of God.

1. He leads them to the cross of Christ.

2. He leads them to the throne of grace.

3. He leads them to the volume of the Book.

4. He leads them in the path of duty. Makes it known. Helps them in it.

5. He leads them through the mazes of trial and temptation.

6. He leads them through the valley of the shadow of death.

7. He leads them to Emmanuel's land.

Selected

The Overcomer's Secret

Christ had spoken strongly of the world hating Him. His kingdom and the kingdom of this world were in deadly hostility. John had understood the lesson, and summed up all in the words: "We know that we are of God, and the whole world lieth in wickedness." "Love not the world, nor the things that are of the world. If any man love the world, the love of the Father is not in him. . . ."

Christ left us with the great far-reaching promise: "Be of good cheer, I have overcome the world." As the child of God abides in Christ and seeks to live the heavenly life in the power of the Holy Spirit, he may confidently count on the power to overcome the world. "Who is he that overcometh the world, but he that believeth that Jesus is the Son of God?" "I live by the faith of the Son of God, who loved me, and gave himself for me"; this is the secret of daily, hourly victory over the world and all its secret, subtle temptation. But it needs a heart and a life entirely possessed by the faith of Jesus Christ to maintain the victor's attitude at all times. Put your trust in the mighty power of God, in the abiding presence of Jesus, as the only pledge of certain and continual victory.

Andrew Murray

THE SPIRIT EFFECTIVE IN THE BELIEVER

1 Corinthians 2

1. The **Effective Power.** "Demonstration of the Spirit and of power" (v. 4).

2. The **Effective Revealer**. "But God hath revealed them unto us by his Spirit" (v. 10).

3. The **Effective Searcher**. "The Spirit searcheth all things" (v. 10).

4. The **Effective Knower**. "The things of God knoweth no man, but the Spirit of God" (v. 11).

5. The **Effective Communicator**. "We have . . . the [S]pirit . . . that we might know" (v. 12).

6. The **Effective Teacher**. "The Holy Ghost teacheth" (v. 13).

7. The **Effective Discerner**. "The natural man receiveth not the things of the Spirit of God . . . they are spiritually discerned [discerned by the Spirit] . . . we have the mind of Christ" (vv. 14–16).

F. E. Marsh

He Must Do It

When I do it, faith is lacking,
   And ambition takes me through;
I promote if for my glory,
   By myself His work I do.
If He does it, I am nothing,
   Just a channel, nothing more,
He the Worker, I the agent,
   This I covet and implore.
He must do it, oh, to let Him!
   If I'm yielded to His will
Whether then success or failure,
All is well, and naught is ill.

Oswald J. Smith

SOWING AND REAPING

But this I say, He which soweth sparingly shall reap also sparingly; and he which soweth bountifully shall reap also bountifully (2 Cor. 9:6).

The Scriptures abound in a great variety of most beautiful images and figurative allusions. This meaningful figure of seed sowing is one. A good deed is a seed that will go on multiplying forever.

Some well-known principles of planters are applicable to our spiritual lives.

I. What We Reap Depends upon What We Sow.

"Do men gather grapes of thorns, or figs of thistles?" (Matt. 7:16). "He that soweth to his flesh shall of the flesh reap corruption; but he that soweth to the Spirit shall of the Spirit reap life everlasting." "Whatsoever a man soweth that shall he also reap" (Gal. 6:8).

II. The Amount We Reap Depends Largely upon the Amount We Sow.

"He which soweth sparingly," etc. People who put little into their Christian living do not get much out of it.

III. Therefore to Get Much Out of Our Faith We Must Put Much into It.

A. Not merely money, but life, talent, time, personality, service. "Give, and it shall be given unto you" (Luke 6:38).

B. There are too many bargain hunters in the church. They want most for the least. They want the benefits of religion without the cost. How can we hope to get good out of worship without giving attention? How can we hope to get good out of the Bible if we do not read and apply it? How can we get good from God if we do not pray, if we never ask? To get much out of your faith, put much in.

IV. He Who Sows Bountifully Shall Reap Bountifully!

A glorious reward awaits us now in this life, but even more is promised in the future realm!

Selected

THE SWORD OF THE SPIRIT

And the sword of the Spirit, which is the word of God (Eph. 6:17).

The Christian's life is one of spiritual warfare. He has many foes stronger than he, more subtle, and mostly they are invisible. They also have allies in his own breast, even depraved appetites ready to join in opposition. But our heavenly Father has provided also for our protection. He furnishes every necessary weapon, as this chapter in Ephesians indicates. We are thinking at this moment of the "sword of the Spirit, which is the word of God"—a most ancient and excellent weapon. This Word of God is not only the ground of a Christian's faith and hope, but it is the Sword by which he defends himself or attacks his enemies.

I. Why the Word of God May Be Compared to a Sword.

For one thing, a sword is *a military weapon* with which soldiers are armed, indispensable to every rank and quality. Christ, the Captain of our salvation, fought with this weapon (Matt. 4:4–8); all the soldiers in His army must therefore be armed with it.

The sword is also a *defensive weapon* (Pss. 17:4; 119:92). The apostles used it in defense of the Gospel. It is an honorable weapon and of great antiquity, having been in use from the beginning. It is also an instrument of victory. So is the Word of God (Rev. 12:11).

II. Why Is It Called "the Sword of the Spirit"?

A. Because the Holy Spirit is the Author of it (2 Peter 2:21).

B. Because it is a spiritual weapon, designed to be of use in the spiritual warfare and against our spiritual foes.

C. Because it is the Spirit who gives the word its efficacy—in the soul and in its external application.

The Holy Spirit guides the truth to our souls and fixes it there. The same Holy Spirit makes the Gospel the power of God to salvation throughout the world.

Set a high value upon the Scriptures.

Learn to know the proper use of this spiritual weapon.

Selected

PATIENCE

1 Thessalonians 5:14

Patience, or "longsuffering" as the King James Version has it, is the fourth aspect of the fruit listed in Galatians 5:22–23.

Concerning patience, we need to recognize:

1. God is a God of patience (Rom. 15:5).

2. Christ is set forth as an example of patience (Isa. 53:3–4, 7; Matt. 27:12–14).

3. The prophets and saints of past ages are set forth as examples of patience (James 5:10).

4. Let patience have her perfect work (James 1:4).

5. Patience produces experience (Rom. 5:4).

6. Patience produces hope (Rom. 15:4).

7. To suffer with patience for well-doing is acceptable with God (1 Peter 2:20).

I. Patience May Be Increased:
A. By constant exercise (2 Peter 1:5–8).
B. By passing through deep trials (Rom. 5:3; James 1:3).

II. Patience Should Be Exercised in:
A. Running the Christian race (Heb. 12:1).
B. Bringing forth fruit (Luke 8:15).
C. Well-doing (Gal. 6:9).
D. Waiting for Christ (2 Thess. 3:5).
E. Tribulation (Rom. 12:12).
F. Receiving answers to prayer (Heb. 6:12, 15).

III. Patience Should be Accompanied:
A. By faith (2 Thess. 1:4).
B. With joyfulness (Col. 1:11).

We must "be patient toward all men" (1 Thess. 5:14).

Selected

HOLINESS: HELPS, HINDRANCES, AND HOPES

1 Peter 1:13, 16

I. Holiness.
What is it? Godlikeness.
A. It must stand the test of the world, it judges us keenly, yet we may deceive it by a powerless form of godliness (2 Tim. 3:5) or a fair exterior (1 Sam. 16:7).
B. It must stand the test of our conscience (1 Cor. 4:3–4), but it is possible to be self-deceived (Jer. 17:9).
C. It must stand the test of God (Jer. 17:10); pray (Ps. 1:23–24) and test it in His sight by His Word (Heb. 4:12–13).

II. Helps.
A concentrated mind (Ps. 86:11, 108).
A. Never diverted or distracted by surroundings (Heb. 12:1).
B. A chastened method, be sober in food, dress, and words.
C. A cheerful manner, hope perfectly.
D. A confirmed man, perfect obedience (Heb. 5:8).

III. Hindrances.
A. Lawlessness (Eph. 5:6).
B. Lovelessness (Rev. 2:4–5).
C. Lustfulness (James 1:13, 15).

IV. Hopes.
A. To be holy, like God.
B. A command, "Ye shall be holy" (1 Pet. 1:16 ASV).

Everywhere—in church, business, the street, holidays, home, and heart, we are to show whose we are and whom we serve. Without the indwelling Holy Spirit, this would be impossible!

Tools for the Master's Work

THE COMMITTED LIFE

1 Peter 4:19

Introduction

    A. At this verse Peter reaches the climax of the lengthy exhortation begun at 2:1. In the KJV it begins with "wherefore," and so this verse concludes the exhortation with it. The word expresses here a great climax, a general conclusion, and a glorious counsel.

    B. This verse has been a great comfort and consolation to many a severely tested and troubled soul. Its formula for victory is simple and certain. And underlying it all is the assurance only the Holy Spirit can give.

I. Seek God's Will Even If You Must Suffer for It.

    A. God does not wish suffering for the sake of suffering merely.

        1. If we suffer, let suffering perform its redemptive purpose in our lives, i.e., to make us like Christ.

        2. If we suffer, let us go on doing right. Cf. MOFFATT's translation. Surrender to God's will does not mean careless indolence, but the active practice of good.

        3. If we suffer, let it be for a good cause and in a right spirit. Cf. Wesley's notes.

    B. God does not wish sin.

        1. God puts a premium on "well doing." Note the many emphases on "well doing" and "good works" in this epistle: 2:12, 15, 20; 3:11, 13, 17; 4:19. Plus the urgency of a good conscience, 3:16, 21.

        2. God opposes all sins, either of the flesh or of the spirit. Cf. 2:1, 11; 3:3, 12; 4:3, 15.

    C. God prefers suffering to sinning.

II. Commit Your Soul to God's Keeping Power.

    A. Here we must follow Christ's example (see 2:23; Luke 23:46).

    B. Here we must have a concern for the greater values. Be sure the soul is committed to God, regardless of what may befall the body (Matt. 10:28).

    C. Here is the sacred deposit of a Christian. Do good and trust God with the consequences. God is able to guard what we have committed to Him. This is a banking figure of speech. Guard our deposit (2 Tim. 1:12). Never fear the outcome of righteousness.

III. Count on God's Faithfulness to All His Creatures.
    A. Great is God's faithfulness.
        1. Contrast this with man's fickleness.
        2. In His truth, love, and power—we may safely trust (Isa. 40:28).
    B. Great is God's creatorship (cf. Neh. 9:6; Isa. 45:12; Heb. 11:3; Rev. 4:11). As divine Creator, He perfectly understands the needs of all His creatures and provides for all. We are the offspring of God (Acts 17:28–29).
    C. Great is God's solicitude.
        1. God is not indifferent to our sufferings.
        2. He who minds the sparrow's fall and numbers each hair of one's head has a concern for your well-being (Luke 12:7; 1 Peter 5:7).
        3. He is still the Eternal Father (Matt. 6:32–33; 7:11; 2 Peter 2:9). God cares!

Conclusion
    A. If we will be faithful in "well doing" and unfaltering in our commitment to God, God will guard faithfully our eternal well-being.
    B. This verse is the great exhortation to sufferers, the divine subjunctive to Christians, and the apostolic summation of the believer's hope.
    C. This is the foundation stone of life's ultimate confidence.

Ross E. Price
The Preacher's Magazine

Sowing and Reaping

In spite of sorrow, loss, and pain,
    Our course be onward still;
We sow on Burma's barren plain,
    We reap on Zion's hill.

Adoniram Judson

JOY OF THE LORD

Nehemiah 8:10

Joy is another of the sometimes misunderstood facets of the fruit of the Spirit. The joy *of* the Lord, not our joy *in* Him, is our strength.

1. The joy of the Lord's **compassion** is our strength in testimony as we remember we are saved by Him (Luke 15:1–7).

2. The joy of the Lord's **treasure** (which is His people) is our strength in Christian life as we recognize we are His property (Matt. 12:44).

3. The joy of the Lord's **Cross** is our strength in persecution as we consider Him in prayerful meditation through His Word (Heb. 12:1, 3).

4. The joy of the Lord's **oneness** with us is our strength in fruit-bearing as we abide in Him (John 15:11).

5. The joy of His **presence** is our strength in our walk as we look to Him in faith (Ps. 105:43).

6. The joy of His **joy** is our strength in communion as we have fellowship with Him (Zeph. 3:16–17).

7. The joy of His **presentation** and **commendation** shall be our strength in glory to praise Him for all His grace given (Jude 24).

F. E. Marsh

It Is Well with My Soul

When peace, like a river, attendeth my way, when sorrows like sea billows roll—Whatever my lot, Thou hast taught me to say, It is well with my soul.

Tho Satan should buffet, tho trials should come, let this blest assurance control, that Christ hath regarded my helpless estate and shed His own blood for my soul.

And, Lord, haste the day when my faith shall be sight, the clouds be rolled back as a scroll: The trump shall resound and the Lord shall descend, "Even so"— it is well with my soul.

Horatio G. Spafford

A SPIRITUAL CHART

Thou art lukewarm, and neither cold nor hot (Rev. 3:16).

Today we have physical charts and mental charts. This Scripture suggests the possibility of charting ourselves spiritually. Each church member may place himself in one of three classes—hot, lukewarm, or cold; active, inactive, or dead.

I. Church attendance (stewardship of time).

A. Active ("not forsaking the assembling of yourselves together").

B. Inactive (lukewarm). Attend irregularly. Go when convenient.

C. Dead (cold). Take no interest in church attendance.

II. Giving to the Lord (stewardship of money).

A. Active (1 Cor. 16:2). Give regularly "upon the first day of the week"; systematically, "as God hath prospered him."

B. Inactive (lukewarm). Give "off and on," when convenient. Give with reluctance, perhaps grumble about it.

C. Dead (cold). Refuse to give at all.

III. Service (stewardship of life).

A. Active (hot). ("Present your body a living sacrifice.") Care for religious duties as faithfully as for secular. Assume responsibility for some particular task and do it cheerfully.

B. Inactive (lukewarm). They pull by jerks. Accept responsibility, but fail in crisis.

C. Dead (cold). Use church for funeral purposes only. If monthly grade chart were used they would receive zero. Let each one honestly mark his own chart.

Selected

THE UNITY OF THE SPIRIT

*Endeavouring to keep the unity of the Spirit in the bond
of peace (Eph. 4:3).*

Introduction

Paul's plea to the Ephesians was most tender. He was a prisoner
in Rome for the Gospel's sake. He therefore reminds them of this:
"I therefore, the prisoner of the Lord," etc. (v. 1). He urges a walk of
Christian holiness, etc., worthy of their profession. He then pre-
sents the spirit they are to cherish toward each other (v. 2). Four
things, and all to be cherished in "love." Then he presses on them
the necessity of "endeavouring to keep the unity of the spirit," etc.

Notice,

I. The Unity Existing.

You cannot keep what you don't possess; this unity, therefore, was a reality, a fact.

But observe,

A. It was not *uniformity* of which he *speaks*. This did not,
nor ever can exist. It is seen nowhere. Diversity, variety everywhere.
Trees, plants, flowers, creatures. So in the human species, color,
size, etc. So of angels. But it was,

B. *Unity.* Now varied plants belong to one order. All men
have this unity physically. "God has made," etc. Human oneness,
erectness, brain, heart, general system the same. So in God's children. One spiritual nature, one body in Christ, members one of another. One vine, one temple, etc. This exists as a divine result—we
cannot make it nor hinder it.

C. This *unity* is *spiritual.* By the Spirit, of the Spirit, having
the Spirit. "The Spirit beareth witness," etc. "Because we are sons
of God," etc. "If any man have not the Spirit," etc. The same Spirit
calls, convinces, renews, witnesses, sanctifies, comforts, guides, etc.

D. This *unity* is *universal.* Over the world—in all ages, coun-
tries, colors, tongues, sects, etc. But the apostle obviously assumes,

II. That This Existing Unity May Be Broken.

It may be broken:

A. *Outwardly*. So Paul distinctly states (1 Cor. 3:1–3). Sectarianism breaks it—tears the Savior's robe—partitions off the church, etc. It may be broken,

B. *Inwardly*. By envying, strifes, evil surmisings. Selfishness breaks it, spiritual pride breaks it, anger and bitterness break it, unforgiveness breaks it. Now both the inward and outward unity may be broken, and hence exclusiveness and hatred are the result. But the apostle,

III. Impresses upon Us the Course We Should Take.

"Endeavouring to keep the unity," etc. Now there is to be put forth,

A. *Real effort*. "Endeavouring." Seek it, live for it, labor for it, pray for it, cherish it.

B. It must be *meek* and *humble effort*. Not boisterous, loud, dogmatic; but calm, quiet, etc.

C. It must be *forbearing effort*. Others may differ, but it may be the result of ignorance, prejudice, education, divers influences, etc. Now bearance with their infirmities and forbearance must be cultivated.

D. It must be *constant effort*. Perils and difficulties constant—a part of our creed, profession, experience, and practice, and that daily.

E. It must be divine *relying effort*. Looking to the grace of God—trusting in the divine aid. Not in our own spirit or strength, but in the Lord's.

Conclusion

Now the application of the subject may supply us with motives:

A. Our own well-being. This unity is our adorning, our comfort, and our growth.

B. This unity honors the divine Spirit. He seeks to work this in us. He is glorified by it.

C. It answers the great prayer of the Savior—His last, etc. (John 17).

D. It is the power of the church of Christ.

E. It will be the grand attraction of those without.

Jabez Burns

WHEN THE PARACLETE COMES
(PENTECOST)

At that day ye shall know (John 14:20).

When Jesus referred to "that day," He meant that on any day when any men anywhere turn from self-will and yield themselves completely to the ever-present Spirit, such men shall know. But what shall men then know? The answer is that they shall know just what the early disciples came to know.

1. They Knew the Way.

There came a new sense of direction. They saw clearly that the King's highway was not a military road of might and power, where swords flashed and chariots rolled, but the lowly path of ministry to others.

2. They Knew the Truth.

Not all at once, of course. But there came an illumination that pierced the bandages of tradition covering their eyes, so that their darkness was changed to light and their perplexed groping to firm assurance.

3. They Knew Life.

Not by the testimony of others, but by personal experience they came to realize what Jesus had tried in vain to teach them, that "eternal life" did not mean only a future life in another world, but a higher, Spirit-filled life in this world.

4. They Knew Power.

Spiritual resources within themselves; the invincible might of the indwelling God; the ability to achieve the impossible.

5. They Knew Fellowship.

Such as never before known. It was fellowship with God and one another.

6. They Knew Their Task.

They knew the high calling wherewith they were called. So they began and continued to manifest the new life, to use their enhanced powers, in order to make known to others what they knew.

J. E. Clarke

BY MY SPIRIT

Zechariah 4:7

I. A Task Declared.
A. A divinely appointed task.
B. A task with kingdom implications.

II. A Man Employed.
A. Called of God—a great honor.
B. Entrusted by God—a great responsibility.
C. Essential in the divine plan.
D. "The man" is usually a young man.
   Moses, Joseph, David, Paul, and Jesus Christ.

III. The Power Released.
A. Never to be sought apart from God.
B. How obtained?
   1. By personal devotion—Gideon at worship under difficulty.
   2. By immediate obedience carefully carried out. Gideon obeyed according to detailed instruction.
   3. By faith in God. Torches and trumpets indicate faith.

Fred Reedy

With infinite care and forethought God has chosen the best place in which you can do your best work for the world. You may be lonely, but you have no more right to complain than the lamp has, which has been placed in a niche to illumine a dark landing or a flight of dangerous stone steps. The master of the house may have put you in a very small corner and on a very humble stand, but it is enough if it be His blessed will. Some day He will pass by, and you shall light His steps as He goes forth to seek and save that which is lost; or you shall kindle some great light that shall shine like a beacon over the storm-swept ocean. Thus the obscure Andrew was the means of igniting his brother Peter when he brought him to Jesus.

Selected

PENTECOST: THE COMING OF THE HOLY SPIRIT

Acts 2:1–4

Introduction

Contextual

I. The Holy Spirit Was Promised.
A. By Joel (Joel 2:28).
B. By John (Matt. 3:11–12).
C. By Jesus (John 14:16).

II. Preparation for the Holy Spirit's Coming.
A. Expectancy
B. Obedience to the Lord's command to tarry (Acts 1:4).
C. Unity (Acts 2:1).
D. Prayer (Acts 2:1).

III. The Holy Spirit's Coming.
A. It was an instantaneous experience.
B. Their hearts were purified (Acts 2:3; 15:8–9).
C. They were filled with the Holy Spirit (Acts 2:4).

IV. The Results of the Holy Spirit's Coming.
A. A new dispensation was ushered in.
B. The disciples received power (Acts 1:8).
   1. Power for victorious living.
   2. Power for witnessing.
   3. Power for service.

Conclusion

If Jesus was anxious that the disciples, whom He was leaving, tarry for this experience, how much we too need to tarry until endued with power from above. We are still in the dispensation of the Holy Spirit. Let us tarry until we have our personal Pentecost. We need it today.

Carl Allen

THE VINE AND THE BRANCHES

I am the true vine, [etc.] (John 15:1–8).

If we think of the Holy Spirit as the vine and Christians as the branches, and the fruit of the Spirit as the outgrowth of godly living, this picture of the vine and the branches takes on new and imperative meaning.

1. **A Blessed Relation (v. 5).**
   Requires both to make the perfect vine. This relation organic.

2. **A Worthy Purpose ("bear fruit").**
   The vine cannot bear fruit without the branches. Our responsibility for giving to the world the fruitage of Christ's life.

3. **A Lofty Motive ("my Father glorified").**
   Not for the vine, or the branch, but for the husbandman. "That they may see your good works," etc.

4. **A Vital Condition ("abide").**
   The unity of life. The idea of self-sufficiency is suicidal. "Apart from me . . . nothing."

5. **A Solemn Warning ("cast forth," etc.).**
   No place in God's economy for anything useless. Anything that is useless is harmful. The unfruitful branch saps the strength of the vine.

6. **A Faithful Helper ("the husbandman").**
   What a beautiful picture of God's watchful interest and care! "Cleanseth." Insects that suck the life and useless shoots that waste energy. God takes away from us only that which is harmful.

7. **A Blessed Assurance ("ask what ye will . . .").**
   Anything in harmony with the purposed producing of fruit. All the strength and vitality needed.

Selected

OFFICES OF THE HOLY SPIRIT

John 16:8–11

I. To Convince the World of Sin: The sin of rejecting Christ was that which the Spirit was more particularly to reveal to the world.

A. This office the Spirit exercised among the Jews.

B. And He discovered it fully by His miraculous operations on the disciples.

C. This office too He yet executes in the Christian church.

1. The external testimony that He gave remains the same in all ages.

2. The internal witness is given to those only whom "God has ordained to life."

II. To Convince the World of Righteousness: that Christ was a righteous Person, and that through His righteousness others also might be saved.

A. He shows to the soul the suitableness and all-sufficiency of Christ's righteousness to all those who trust in it (v. 14).

B. And leads them, with holy glorying to say, "In the Lord have I righteousness and strength" (Isa. 45:24).

III. To Convince the World of Judgment: He showed to the first Christians that Satan was a vanquished foe.

A. By the descent of the Spirit it was manifest that Christ had triumphed over sin and Satan, death and hell (Eph. 4:8; Col. 2:15).

B. By His gracious influences also He rescued myriads from their power—and inspired them with a holy confidence that they should finally prevail over all their spiritual enemies (2 Tim. 1:12).

C. However active and malicious Satan is, his head is bruised (Gen. 3:15), his power is limited (1 Peter 5:8; Rev. 2:10), his doom is fixed (Rom. 16:20).

Application

A. Of conviction:

1. All true Christians have received the Spirit for the ends and purposes for which He is here promised.

2. In vain then will be our orthodoxy in sentiment, if we have not this evidence of our conversion to God.

B. Of consolation:
 1. Are we bowed down with a *sense* of sin? We may be
    sure that Christ has sent His Spirit to work that
    conviction in us; and that, if we be instant in prayer,
    He will, by the same Spirit, lead us also to a view of
    His righteousness.
 2. Are we ready to despond by reason of the *power* of
    sin? The resistance which the Holy Spirit has
    enabled us already to make to its dominion is a
    pledge that "we shall be more than conquerors . . ."
    (Rom. 8:37).

adapted from Charles Simeon

There is no order so holy, nor place so secret, where there are not
temptations, or adversities. There is no man who is altogether safe
from temptations while he lives on earth; for in ourselves is the root
of temptation, in that we are born in the desire of evil.

Thomas à Kempis